Ian Jubb's
EXETER
Collection

Other Books in this Series
Albert Labbett's Crediton Collection
Albert Labbett's Crediton Collection II
An Alphington Album, *P. Aplin & J. Gaskell*
The Dawlish Collection, *Bernard Chapman*
The Totnes Collection, *Bill Bennett*
Pictures of Paignton, *Peter Tully*
Pictures of Paignton Part II, *Peter Tully*
Dartmoor in Colour, *Chips Barber*
Exeter in Colour, *Chips Barber*
Torbay in Colour, *Chips Barber*
Plymouth in Colour, *Chips Barber*

For further details of these or any of our extensive Devon titles, please contact us at 2 Church Hill, Pinhoe, Exeter, EX4 9ER, Tel: (0392) 68556.

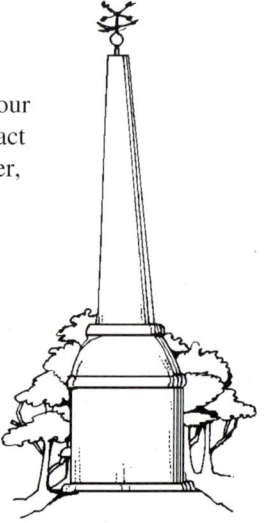

ISBN: 0 946651 68 X

Other Obelisk Publications
The Lost City of Exeter, *Chips Barber*
Diary of a Dartmoor Walker, *Chips Barber*
Diary of a Devonshire Walker, *Chips Barber*
Adventure Through Red Devon, *R. B. Cattell*
Under Sail Thr S Devon & Dartmoor, *R. B. Cattell*
The Great Walks of Dartmoor, *Terry Bound*
The A to Z of Dartmoor Tors, *Terry Bound*
The Great Little Dartmoor Book, *Chips Barber*
The Great Little Exeter Book, *Chips Barber*
Made in Devon, *Chips Barber & David FitzGerald*
Tales of the Unexplained in Devon, *Judy Chard*
Haunted Happenings in Devon, *Judy Chard*
Dark & Dastardly Dartmoor, *Sally & Chips Barber*
Weird & Wonderful Dartmoor, *Sally & Chips Barber*
Ghastly & Ghostly Devon, *Sally & Chips Barber*
The Ghosts of Exeter, *Sally & Chips Barber*
Ten Family Walks on Dartmoor, *Sally & Chips Barber*
Ten Family Walks in East Devon, *Sally & Chips Barber* (Harback)
More... Cobblestones Cottages & Castles, *David Young*

First Published in 1993 by Obelisk Publications
2 Church Hill, Pinhoe, Exeter, Devon
Designed by Chips and Sally Barber
Typeset by Sally Barber
Printed in Great Britain by
Sprint Print Co Ltd, Okehampton Place, Exeter

© **Ian Jubb 1993**
All Rights Reserved

Exeter's cathedral dominates the skyline from many vantage points. Even from the air it stands out as the major city landmark. In the top left of this old aerial picture the line of Georgian buildings is the former Royal Devon and Exeter Hospital. The High Street runs along the lower third of the photo, Queen Street joining it close to the word 'air'. There is no Western Way in the top right as it did not exist when this bird's eye view of Exeter was taken!

Here we have two views of an Exeter church which no longer exists. St Mary Major was rebuilt in 1865 following in the wake of earlier churches on the same site. In fact an original building is recorded in 1050, long before the Cathedral started to take on its present appearance. It is believed that John Wesley preached here on the morning of Sunday, 24 November 1739. However he was banned from preaching that afternoon as the rector regarded his doctrines as "dangerous"! When the church was demolished, Roman Baths were found beneath it and what to do about them has fuelled many an animated discussion. Picture postcards with St Mary Major in all its glory continued to be sold long after it had been demolished. The cross which sat atop its spire still exists, planted in the grass immediately below where it once stood. On its concrete mount it reveals that the church was demolished in 1971.

Lots of people walk through The Globe Hotel daily, even though it has long gone! (It was a victim of Hitler's bombers.) The tallest part of this fine hotel is now the point where it is possible to walk from the Cathedral area through to the top of South Street, emerging by the traffic lights.

This is one of my most prized postcards and shows a very different South Street to the one we see today. Instead of the seemingly never-ending streams of traffic penned back by the traffic lights at the top of the street, we have a more relaxed thoroughfare with people as happy to walk in the roadway as stroll along on the pavements.

The caption clearly states that this is Fore Street and that is true as far down as the junction on the right with Bartholomew Street. Below this is Bridge Street and the beginning of Exe Bridge can just be spied in the distance.

8

On the left of page 8 is St Mary Arches Church which gives its name to the street. When this picture was taken there were no cars and the road was only half its present width. Beside it is a picture of Chevalier House which was just around the corner, almost opposite the present site of British Home Stores at the top of Fore Street. 'Chevalier' is the French word for knight and for years a model of a knight on horseback, just visible on the top of the right gable, stood sentinel.

Above are the almshouses at the back of the former Episcopal Secondary School near St Michael's Church in the St David's area of Exeter. In years gone by pupils from the school would distribute produce from their Harvest Festival to the elderly residents of these almshouses, "Exeter Free Houses" built in the 1860s. The fountain is still there though the seat and its occupant have gone!

Exeter's High Street when the electric trams were the main form of transport apart from the occasional car!

Another High Street view but further up the street and many years later! On the right W.H. Smith's previous shop can be seen. Above the J. Lyons & Co. Ltd sign is a bare wall that now features a mural portraying three characters which have an historic Exeter connection – Thomas Bodley, Nicholas Hilliard and Princess Henrietta Ann.

Boots used to be on the corner of Queen Street where C & A is today, as is evident from this picture. On the opposite side was Walton's, a store which served the people of Exeter very well for a great many years. Today Marks and Spencer occupy the site.

The Victoria Hall in Queen Street was a popular place of entertainment in Edwardian Exeter. Films were shown in summer (West's Animated Pictures) whilst dances were held in winter. Alas this small version of London's Albert Hall was burnt down. The picture shows the crowd which gathered to watch the proceedings.

(Above) This is not a very old picture but it serves to show how change can take place even in one of the more modern-looking streets. Double decker buses and other traffic used it as a through route for years before steps were taken to send motorists off on more roundabout ways of getting around the city.

(Right) The entrance to this fine arcade stood almost opposite the present Boots store at East Gate. It was just one of many fine features of Exeter which were destroyed in times of war.

This postcard view was sent to Tiverton, postmarked 15 May 1905, about six weeks after the introduction of electric trams to Exeter. Great crowds gathered along the High Street to welcome this revolutionary form of transport to the city.

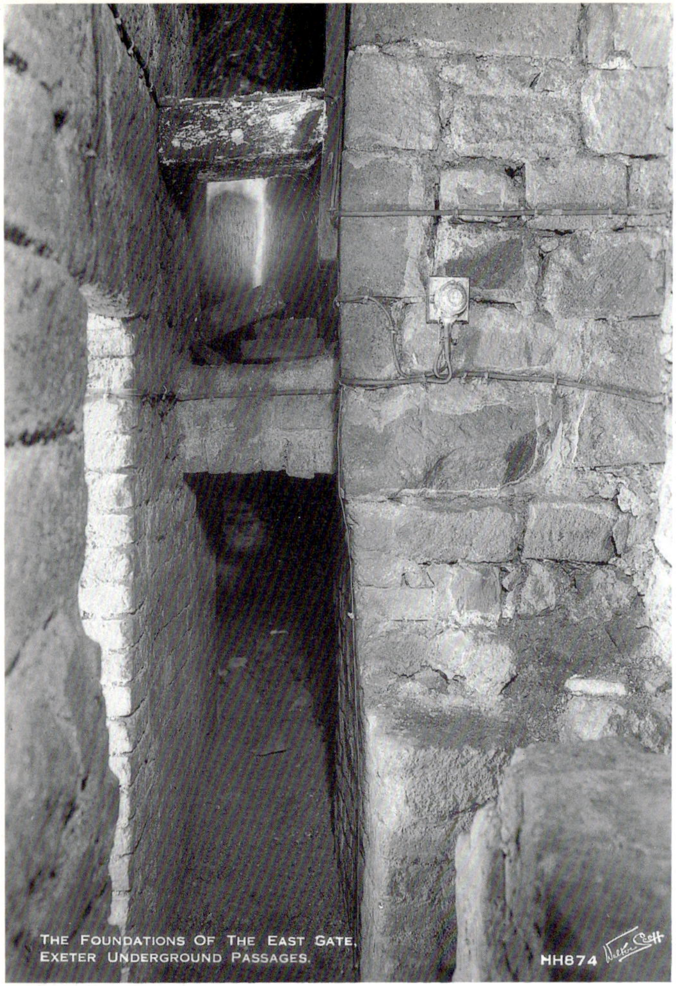
THE FOUNDATIONS OF THE EAST GATE.
EXETER UNDERGROUND PASSAGES.
HH874

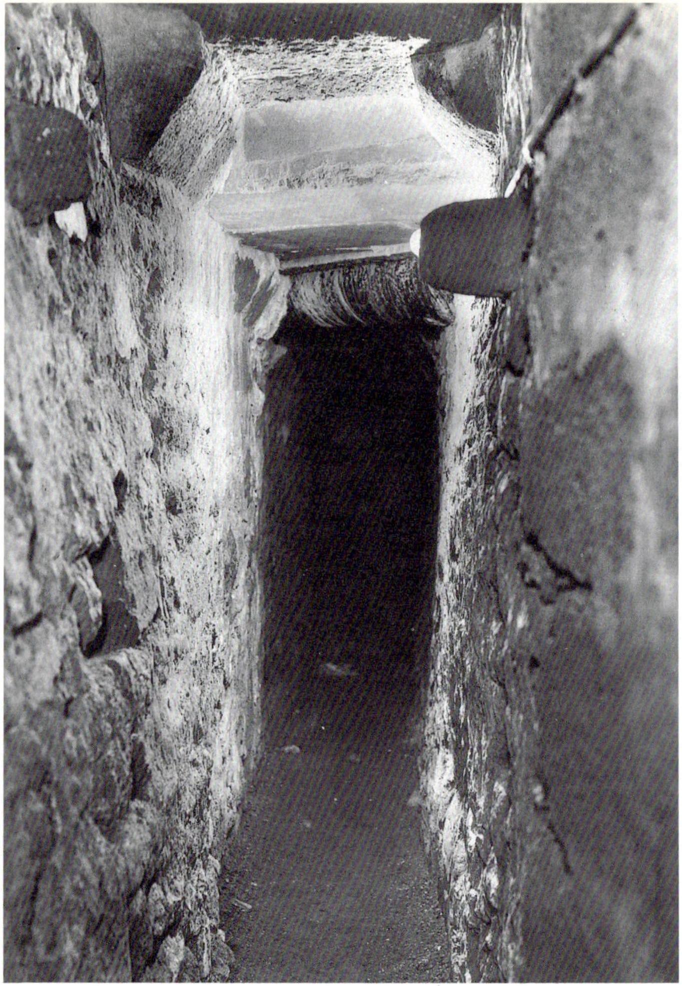

Exeter's medieval underground passages are now an important tourist attraction and still look very much the same as they did many years ago when these photographs were taken. They were constructed to carry water from a series of strong, sparkling springs which were located outside the city wall, just beyond East Gate, more or less where Debenhams store is located today. A new entrance to these passages, together with shop, has been constructed beside Boots and informative guided tours of these subterranean waterways are possible – except when they are flooded after heavy downpours of rain! It is a fact that visitors are more likely to go down than locals even though most Exonians say that they will go 'one day'! Provided you don't suffer from claustrophobia, you should enjoy a visit to this most unusual of tourist attractions.

The New London Hotel no longer exists, but when it did it was in London Inn Square, an area at the junction of Sidwell Street and High Street. To the left of the hotel is Northernhay Place, much of the left side of which still looks very much like it does today. At the top is the gate to Northernhay Gardens. To the right, a short distance away, is the Theatre Royal ...

Exeter. Longbrook Street.

The Theatre Royal was a distinct landmark on the junction of New North Road and Longbrook Street until 1962. It had the great misfortune to suffer the worst theatre fire in history, within a year of its opening, in which a total of 186 people perished. The tragedy occurred on 5 September 1887 leaving 98 children orphaned. On a lighter note, motorists approaching this forking of the ways must have travelled much more slowly in the past as the sign on the lamppost, pointing to "Tiverton, Barnstaple and Crediton", could only have been read from a matter of yards!

Sidwell Street long before the days it was lined with stalls. This view is taken looking up the street. The tree on the left marks the entrance to St Sidwell's Church.

EXETER, SIDWELL STREET

This is taken further up the street close to the junction of York Road. Notice The Acland Arms on the left hand side where a petrol station is now located. This pub was originally called The Mail Coach but then changed to The Turk's Head before adopting the name of one of Devon's most famous families, the Aclands.

This is our last picture of Sidwell Street in bygone days. It is a lasting reminder of what it was like when it had a much greater variety of architectural styles than the present street.

Another famous local family were the Bampfyldes whose main country residence was Poltimore House some four miles from the centre of Exeter. Although they owned much property, they sold this late sixteenth century house to some coal merchants – Messrs Varwell, Guest and Co. In 1933 it was bought by the city council but nine years later, in 1942, it was destroyed in a wartime raid. It stood on the corner of Bampfylde Street and Catherine Street.

Belmont Park as it was in 1912. Since then there have been many more activities for youngsters to enjoy in the area on the middle right of the photo. The trees which have survived the years are now much more mature and behave accordingly!

I have seen this particular postcard reproduced on many occasions but I don't think it has ever looked as clear or sharp as this! It shows The Old Pinhoe Turnpike Gate which was situated just above the traffic lights at Mount Pleasant. The Mount Pleasant Inn is directly behind the coach and horses as is a little man carrying a shovel – but he can't be seen!

It is always a bit surprising to see what views end up as postcards! After all, a seaside prom is one thing, but a shot of Whipton Village Road is really something completely different. Here a Whiteway's Cyder lorry is shown outside The Whipton Inn whilst a range of cycles and motor cycles are trustingly parked awaiting the return of their owners. How times have changed!

The Isolation Hospital, Exeter.

This is or was The Isolation Hospital on the outskirts of Whipton. The reason for the uncertainty is that it does not fulfil that particular role today but its buildings have been greatly altered to become the Mickelwright Centre, wedged between the aptly named Hospital Lane and Whipton Barton Road. Beyond the gentleman on the left, at the top of the road, is the Exeter By-pass.

MR CODY AT EXETER.

Samuel Franklin Cody was an Anglo-American aviation pilot who was born in Texas (USA, not the D-I-Y shop!) but who took British nationality in 1909. Here he is seen at Whipton ready for another daredevil flight – the next stage of The Around Britain Air Race. The date is 27 July 1911, the destination is Salisbury in Wiltshire. Just two years later he was killed when one of his bizarre looking machines crashed. This one was nicknamed "The Cathedral".

Meanwhile, back in the relatively quiet backwaters of Heavitree, life went on at a slower pace. South Lawn Terrace hasn't changed a great deal since but the road has now got a better surface and is much wider. The shop on the corner has had various owners but people still think of it as a Shaul Bakery even though another business occupies the premises now. Heavitree School is just about discernible behind the lamppost.

This is Church Street in Heavitree. The shop on the left has been more recently occupied by "Westward Rentals". Note how in these pre-television days quite a healthy little crowd has gathered to watch the photographer at work. Just beyond and to the right of the two ladies is the sheltered homes complex of The Maltings, built on the site of the former Heavitree Brewery.

The Mote Service does a roaring trade today but look how it all began! This was regarded as a plush petrol station when this photo was taken in the pioneer days of motoring.

This picture is taken in the lower part of Fore Street, Heavitree and captures two very different forms of transport heading in opposite directions – the electric tram to St Thomas and the horse and cart on its way out of Heavitree. Regent Square can be seen on the left with The Royal Oak just below it. A little boy is peering up the hill to see what the photographer is doing. Again the card is sent in 1905 so the tram is new and an obvious attraction.

There is only one thing better than a pint at The Royal Oak in Heavitree – and that's two pints! The building on the right has gone and public conveniences are there now. As the brewery was just up the hill, the beer didn't have to travel too far!

This military hospital was in Butts Road where the Territorials have their headquarters. The message on the back of this postcard suggests it was sent by a soldier recuperating from wounds or injuries sustained in combat during the First World War. Postmarked April 1918, the message read: "One of the nicest places in Exeter! I left a few good friends behind when I had to leave."

People still ask for "Heavitree Bridge" when travelling by bus to the Honiton Road end of Rifford Road, even though the bridge shown in the picture has long since gone. The bridge straddled a stream which started on the hills above Whipton and Beacon Heath. In periods of heavy rain it was always prone to flood at this spot because the volume of water trying to pass beneath was too great. As this was such an important route into Exeter, the stream was culverted and the bridge removed. The cottages have also gone.

From something that was there but has gone, to something which wasn't there but now is! The riddle is solved by stating that this old photo of the St Mary Steps area, a familiar view for those who regularly use Western Way, is lacking one of Exeter's most famous buildings – "The House That Moved". This was a few hundred yards away at the time and didn't arrive on this scene until the early 1960s.

There have been several bridges at this point on the River Exe at different times. This was the 1905 version which was designed to permit an easy crossing of the river for the new electric trams. The previous bridge had been one of the humpback type but changing demands necessitated a broader structure. This 'New' bridge was dismantled in the early 1970s and replaced by two new bridges. However the traffic still manages to keep them pretty busy.

On the opposite side of the Exe, in the centre of the picture, is The Fountain Inn which became The Prospect Inn in the late 1950s. A lot of the houses behind the inn, to its left, have gone. Now a strangely out-of-character lift rises and falls in the gap between the two tall warehouses – a reflection of the "ups and downs" of Exeter's Quayside area.

This is the start of the Exeter Canal at King's Arms Sluice. The Cathedral can be spied peeping over the trees to the left of centre with the Georgian row of Colleton Crescent to the left of that. The building on the right of the canal has gone as have all the trees which once gave this scene a much more rural feel.

River Exe in flood Jan 1918.

The Exe regularly flooded the low lying parts of Exeter in the past. Many people recall the floods of 1960 but this picture is from January 1918, taken at the bottom of Weirfield Road below St Leonard's Church. The shop on the corner has gone and two-storey flats have replaced the terraced houses which were here. The Port Royal Inn remains just around the corner to the right.

Stand on Countess Wear Bridge over the River Exe and look towards the city. Today you will see a succession of attractive houses with gardens that go down to the river's edge. When this view was taken there were but a handful of buildings as suburban Exeter was almost non existent. Countess Wear House was built in the seventeenth century and, complete with sundial, is a grade 2 listed building.

The buildings on the left stood where the St Thomas Sainsbury store is today. This part of Alphington Street has changed greatly because it was on the approaches to Exe Bridge. The ever increasing flows of traffic resulted in a clearance of many shops and the disappearance of businesses which had been there for generations.

Alphington Road ends at the railway bridge and Alphington Street begins! This 1916 postcard view reveals that the street was once a more tree-lined thoroughfare than it is today.

Although Ide is not strictly a part of Exeter, it has long been a favoured destination for people on Sunday strolls, particularly those who live to the west of the River Exe. Here quite a crowd has appeared but some people have not stayed still for the photograph so are blurred!

Centre of Village, Ide.

This picture, taken further up Ide's High Street, is more typical with not a soul in sight. There used to be several shops but now there is only the post office and store which is by the telegraph post on the left.

The Lamb Inn in Exwick is still there although its clientele are dressed a little differently these days and its name is now the Village Inn. It was one of the inns used by railway staff from nearby St David's Station – one of them can be seen posing for this photograph. The roof of the former Exwick School can be seen further up the road on the left. To the right of that there are now houses built in Exwick Road.

HOOPERN FIELDS, EXETER.

This is one of the more unusual pictures in the collection for, on face value, there does not appear too much of interest in it. However, all the far hillside is now covered by the buildings of The University of Exeter. For several decades these fields were the chosen rendezvous for courting couples blissfully unaware of what was to happen to these fields beyond the city limits. It is a reminder that places which are now open fields or rolling countryside might well end up at the mercy of the developer!

We finish our nostalgic little romp around Exeter and its environs with a street scene which is instantly recognisable as Blackall Road. The houses are festooned in ivy and now poor old 'ivy' has gone. These were large town houses occupied by families, not "Guest House" or "Bedsit Land" like it is today! The photo is taken from the junction with New North Road, near Prison Lane. Parking problems did not exist for the horse-drawn wagon of Colson and Co., General Drapers, Exeter. Colson's store became the Dingles we know today.